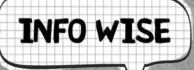

ANALYZE AND DEFINE THE ASSIGNMENT

~Valerie Bodden~

Lerner Publications ◆ Minneapolis

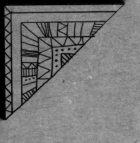

For Josh and our little projects—Hannah, Elijah, Titus, and Chloe

Lerner Publications Company
A division of Lerner Publishing Group, Inc.
241 First Avenue North
Minneapolis, MN 55401 USA

For reading levels and more information, look up this title at www.lernerbooks.com.

Main body text set in Adrianna Regular 11/18. Typeface provided by Chank.

Library of Congress Cataloging-in-Publication Data

Bodden, Valerie.
    Analyze and define the assignment / by Valerie Bodden.
      pages cm — (Info wise)
    Includes index.
    ISBN 978-1-4677-5223-7 (lib. bdg. : alk. paper) — ISBN 978-1-4677-7578-6
    (paperback) — ISBN 978-1-4677-6228-1 (EB pdf)
      1. Report writing—Juvenile literature. 2. Research—Juvenile literature.
  3. Homework—Juvenile literature. 4. Information resources—Juvenile literature.
  I. Title.
  LB1047.3.B63 2015
  371.30281—dc23   2014013256

Manufactured in the United States of America
1 — CG —12/31/14

CONTENTS

INTRODUCTION

INFORMATION DETECTIVES

You've been assigned a research project. *Gulp.* Isn't research what scientists and people at universities do? Well, sure. But it's what you do too, every day, whether you realize it or not.

Research is simply the process of finding and using information to learn something. So every time you jump online to see what movies are playing nearby, you're doing research. Do you turn on the TV to check the weather? That's research too.

Of course, beginning a research project is generally more in-depth than looking up movie listings. But it involves many of the same steps. You need to know what you are looking for. You need to know where you can find it. And then you need to look for it.

Think of it this way: Conducting research is like solving a mystery. The clues you need are out there somewhere, and you get to snoop around until you find the right ones.

Fortunately for you, information is everywhere. It's online. It's in books, magazines, and newspapers. It's even on television, radio, signs, and billboards. So grab your detective cap and get sleuthing!

CHAPTER 1

WHAT AM I DOING?

Like any good detective, you need to know what you are looking for before you can find it. And what you are looking for will depend on the assignment your teacher has given you. Has your teacher asked you to write a report or prepare an oral presentation? Does your teacher want you to make a poster? Are you supposed to get ready for a debate?

Consider what class your assignment is for as well. If you are doing a science project, you may need to conduct an experiment and collect your own data. For reading class, you could read and analyze someone's review of a literary work. For social studies, you might create and then give a survey or conduct an interview. Has your teacher given you any special instructions about the types of sources you need to use? Are you supposed to find a certain number of books? Should you use websites? Are encyclopedias recommended? Will you need to collect your own data? Has your teacher asked you *not* to use a particular source?

PURPOSE

As you think about your assignment, ask yourself what your purpose is in doing it. Sure, you're researching because your teacher says you have to. But any research project has a bigger, more important purpose too.

For some assignments, your purpose is to explain something. For example, your assignment might be to explain recycling. That means you need to describe what recycling is and how it is done.

Instead of explaining, sometimes your purpose is to persuade, or present an argument. If your topic is recycling, you won't just tell about it. You will try to convince your readers to recycle. Or you might argue that recycling programs actually encourage people to produce more waste.

Sometimes you might be asked to compare and contrast two different subjects. Then you need to talk about what is similar between the two topics and what is different. You might compare recycling and waste reduction programs, for example. You could focus on the cost of each. Or perhaps you will compare each program's effects on the environment.

You can figure out the purpose of your research project from the words used to describe the assignment. If your purpose is to explain, your teacher might tell you to *write about something*, to *discuss*, or to *describe*. An assignment for a persuasive paper might ask you to agree or disagree with a strongly worded statement.

Or it might use the words *opinion, think, argue,* or *defend.* A compare-and-contrast project might simply use the words *compare* and *contrast.* Or it might mention *similarities* and *differences.*

Who will read or listen to your completed assignment? Knowing your audience can help you plan your project.

AUDIENCE

As you consider the purpose of your project, also think about your audience. Of course, your teacher is one member of your audience. But will anyone else read, see, or listen to your finished project? If you are giving a presentation in class, your classmates are your audience. The audience for a letter to the editor of a newspaper is the newspaper's readers. The audience for a persuasive project on recycling might be your neighbors. And the audience for a debate or science fair project might include classmates, teachers, parents, or others.

Your audience will affect how you carry out your research. As you think about your audience, consider what they might already know about your topic. What new information can you provide? For a persuasive project, knowing your audience is especially important. If you target your arguments to your audience's specific concerns and outlook, you are more likely to convince them to agree with you or to take action.

If you want to convince your classmates to join a club, for instance, you might focus on the opportunity to make friends and have fun participating in club activities. If, on the other hand, you are trying to convince parents to enroll their children in clubs, you might stress that extracurricular activities strengthen college applications.

If you've reviewed your assignment and you just can't figure out what your purpose is or who your audience might be, ask your teacher to clarify. The same advice is true for any part of the assignment that seems confusing.

WHY AM I DOING THIS?

Sometimes it can be hard to understand why you have to complete a research project. But your teacher has a good reason for assigning it. Most careers require good research skills. Lawyers research historical legal cases related to the ones they're working on. Elected officials (or their assistants) investigate the issues citizens find important. Doctors need to keep up with new studies on health and medical treatments. Video game developers need to find out if someone else has already produced the games they have in mind—or find out what code another designer used to write a really neat aspect of a game. What are your career goals? What kinds of research do you think your future job will require?

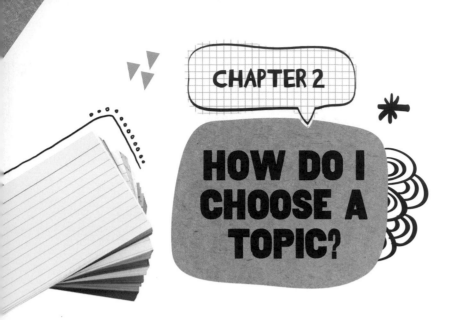

CHAPTER 2

HOW DO I CHOOSE A TOPIC?

Once you're sure you understand your assignment, you need to think about your topic. In some cases, your teacher will give you a specific topic. Then you can move on to the next step. This one has been taken out of your hands.

Often, though, teachers will let you decide on a topic for yourself. Sometimes they might give you a general subject area but let you choose the specific topic within that subject. For example, your teacher might assign you to write a report about an animal but allow you to choose the animal. Or your teacher might say your report has to be about history but let you choose any topic within that broad category. And sometimes your teacher will give you free rein to choose any subject in the world (or out of it!) for your research project.

But there are a lot of subjects in the world. So how do you go about choosing just one? And how do you know if your topic is a good one for a research project?

CONSIDER YOUR INTERESTS

Begin by thinking about your interests. You're going to spend a lot of time on this project. If you pick a topic that doesn't interest you, you're going to get tired of it awfully quickly. And that will make your research project seem more like a chore than like solving a mystery. So don't choose snails when you really want to learn about race cars.

You probably have a lot of interests. If your teacher said your project had to have something to do with the ocean, make a list of everything that interests you about the ocean. Or, if you're free to study any subject you like, you might draw an idea web, like the one below. Your idea web can include any topics and subtopics you find intriguing.

If you have to write a biography, write down the names of all the people you would like to learn more about. When you're done, look back at your list. Do one or two of these people stand out as subjects you'd like to learn more about?

If you can't find a topic by perusing your interests, try browsing online. It can be helpful to start with a subject directory such as the Yahoo! Directory (dir.yahoo.com) or the Internet Public Library (www.ipl.org). Subject directories contain lists of websites organized by subject area. For example, under the general heading *Arts and Humanities,* you might find links for history, literature, and fine art. Clicking on one of those links will take you to an even more specific topic, such as "history of medicine" or "art in the White House."

You might also search for topics by skimming a newspaper or an encyclopedia. Or walk through the library and look for a book that grabs your interest.

Browse for books at your school or local library. What subjects do they cover? Will the topic fit your assignment?

An online subject directory can help you come up with specific subtopics for an overly broad topic.

FIND THE JUST-RIGHT TOPIC

Once you have a potential topic in mind, you need to figure out if it is too broad or too narrow for your assignment. When a topic is too broad, there is too much information about it to fit into one report or project. A topic that can be stated in one word, such as *travel* or *space*, is often too broad. One way to check whether your topic is too broad or too narrow is to do a quick search of your library's online catalog. If more than one hundred books come up, your topic might be too broad. Take the topic of space, for example. A search of just one public library catalog could bring up more than six thousand books. Those could take a while to read! So think about what it is about space that interests you.

If you're really not sure what you want to know more about, read an encyclopedia article about space. Or look up space in an online subject directory. What subtopics are listed? What sections stand

out to you? What would you like to research further? How about stars? Try that in your library catalog. It might cut your results by about half. But three thousand books is still a lot.

Maybe you want to know more about shapes in the stars—constellations. That topic might be specific enough. Or you might want to get even more specific. You could study stories about the constellations. Or you could look into how to spot constellations. You might research how ships' captains used to navigate by looking at constellations. Those are some manageable topics! Another method for narrowing your topic is to limit it to a specific location, time period, or group of people. Instead of researching travel, you might focus on college students who tour Europe after graduation. Or you could research how the automobile impacted travel in the 1920s.

As you work to narrow down your topic, you can add to your idea web. Just make a new cluster for each subtopic you think of. And then make even more specific clusters from those subtopics. Eventually, you should get to a subtopic that is narrow enough—and that interests you!

The opposite problem of a too-broad topic is one that is too narrow. A catalog search might bring up only one or two books on your topic. (Or it may be a topic that isn't covered in books. Then you'll need to check other kinds of sources.)

You can broaden your topic by thinking about the general category it fits into. If you are interested in a clay pot you saw in a museum, you might not be able to find out a lot about that specific

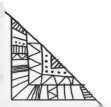

clay pot (unless it's a very famous pot). But if you think more broadly, the pot could fit into the category of pottery or of American Indian art. You could probably find information on the history of the style of pottery you saw in the museum. Or you could research how American Indians made pottery. You might even investigate the physical properties of clay.

How will you know when you have a topic that is just right? You should be able to shape your topic into a specific question, such as "How does Internet advertising target youths aged eight to twelve?" This is your research question. You will ultimately answer it through your research project. You should be able to answer your research question in a single sentence.

Once you have your not-too-broad, not-too-narrow topic picked out, it's time to move on to the next step!

CHAPTER 3

WHAT IS MY RESEARCH PLAN?

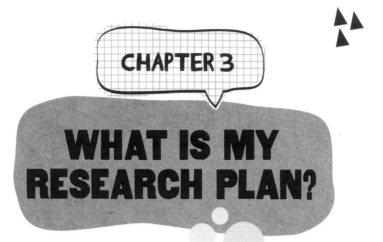

Now that you've gone through all the hard work of picking a topic, you might want to jump right into your research. Your enthusiasm is awesome, but hold on just a little longer! Before you start digging into what other people have to say about your topic, think about what you already know about it—and what you'd like to know.

If your topic is peanut butter, for example, you probably already know that it tastes good. You know it's made out of peanuts. You might also know that some of your friends are allergic to it. But what else would you like to know? Maybe you wonder how exactly peanuts become peanut butter. Are you interested in the history of peanut butter? Perhaps you're wondering why some people are allergic to peanut butter and peanut products.

ALL THE QUESTIONS

Write down a list of questions that you want to answer through your research. As you write questions, consider some common question words.

- *What?* When you ask what something is, you are usually looking for a definition or an explanation. *What is cancer?*
- *Who?* Ask *who* when you want to know more about a person who did something or was affected by something. *Who was displaced by Hurricane Katrina?*
- *Where? Where* questions seek more information about a location. *Where on the moon did* Apollo 11 *land?*
- *When?* Answers to *when* questions involve a time or a duration. *When did women get the right to vote?*
- *How?* Generally, *how* questions can be answered with an explanation or a process. *How does the water cycle work?*
- *Why?* When you ask why, you are asking for an explanation. The question might address cause and effect or the purpose or function of something. *Why do plants need sunlight?*
- *Which? Which* questions often involve comparing and contrasting or making a decision. *Which is better for you: running or swimming?*

Making a list of questions might seem like a lot of extra work. But it will actually save you time in the long run. Thinking about the questions you want to answer will focus your research. It will keep you from spending hours looking at information you don't need.

This does not mean that once you have your questions written, you are done thinking about your topic. Keep an open mind as you research. Finding the answer to one question might lead

When it comes to research questions like "What did Civil War soldiers wear?" photos might be your best source.

to new questions. Add them to the list! Change questions that are too broad or too narrow. Cross out questions that you don't need to answer after all.

Once you have your list of questions, think about the types of information you'll need to answer them. Do you need definitions, examples, or illustrations? What about numbers, such as statistics or dates? Will expert opinions answer your question? If you asked, "When was the Civil War?" you'd need dates to answer your question. "What was the Civil War?" would call for a definition. And to answer "Why was the Civil War fought?" you might look for expert opinions. It might help to make a note after each question about the type of information you will need to answer it.

KEYWORDS ARE THE KEY

You can also use your questions to come up with a list of keywords. These are words you can use in your search for sources. You can use them to search online or in your library's catalog. You can check for them in the indexes of books as well. Look back at your research questions. Write down any important words from the questions. So if your question was "How do dolphins communicate?" you might list *dolphins* and *communication* as keywords. It can also be helpful to list synonyms for your keywords. So you might list *talk* as a synonym for *communicate*. If you have trouble coming up with synonyms, check a thesaurus.

As you're listing keywords, think about related subjects as well. A source on general animal communication might include a section on dolphins. So you might add *animal communication* to your keyword list. If you want to study a specific breed of dolphins, you might add that to your list too. If you've already skimmed an encyclopedia article about the topic, list any important words you found there.

Topic: weather

Preliminary research question: How do people predict the weather?

Keywords: weather, rain, snow, precipitation, temperature, forecast, meteorology, weather radar, weather satellite

THINK ABOUT THE THESIS

As you think about your topic, you might also write a preliminary thesis statement. A thesis statement is a sentence that states the point, or the purpose, of your research project. It is your answer to the research question you posed when choosing and narrowing your topic. A preliminary thesis statement is one that you write early on in your project. It tells what you think the point of your research is going to be.

Go back and look at your research question. Brainstorm some possible answers. Then write your answers as a sentence, with three or four points you want to discuss in your project. For example, say your research question was, "Are standardized tests beneficial to students?" Maybe you don't think they are. In fact, you think they are harmful. Make a list of your reasons.

Then choose the three or four reasons you think are strongest and shape them into a sentence: "Standardized tests are harmful to students because they create unnecessary pressure, encourage teachers to focus on only material that will be on the test, and set up unhealthful competition between students." Of course, you may not know your exact answer to the research question yet. That's okay! The beauty of a preliminary thesis is that it can be changed. So if you find a stronger argument during your research, swap it out! Or if you change your opinion completely, change your thesis too!

Be sure your preliminary thesis is as specific as you can make it. The preliminary thesis "Our country's bridges are scary" is not a specific thesis. But it could be made specific by including information on what you mean by *scary*. A specific preliminary thesis might be the following: "Traveling on bridges in the United States is dangerous because many are more than fifty years old, scheduled bridge inspections are missed, and bridges have begun to fail in recent years."

Your preliminary thesis can be one more tool to help you target your research. It gets you focused on what you need to know to prove your point. But if you don't know a lot about your topic yet, you might want to hold off on writing a preliminary thesis. Do a little research first. Once you have an idea of what you'd like to cover in your project, jot down a preliminary thesis of your own. And speaking of research, let's get to it!

CHAPTER 4

WHAT ARE SOURCES, AND HOW CAN I FIND THEM?

You know your topic. You have some questions to answer. You know what kinds of information you need. You even have some search keywords. What's next?

It's time to start digging for clues. That means starting your preliminary research. Just as your preliminary thesis was an early idea of what your final thesis might be, your preliminary research is an early search of what information about your topic is available. You probably won't use everything you find. But preliminary research can give you an overview of your topic. It can show you if there is enough—or too much—information about your topic and help you narrow your focus further. It might even lead you to change your topic altogether. Better now than when your project is almost complete!

REFERENCE WORKS

Information is everywhere. So where do you start? It may be helpful to start with general sources and work your way to more

specific information. General sources include encyclopedias and other reference works. They can give you an overview of your topic. Reading this overview will make it easier for you to read and understand more specific sources later on. It will also introduce you to any important words used in that subject area. In addition, reading about your topic in a general resource might spark new questions or lead you to examine your topic from a new angle.

Where can you find general resources? Your library probably offers access to online encyclopedias and other reference works. Ask your librarian to teach you how to use them. The library may have print encyclopedias available as well. Your librarian can help you find them.

LIBRARY REFERENCE SOURCES

Libraries can give you access to all kinds of reference sources, both online and in print. You may find some of the following sources useful for your project:

Almanacs: annual compilations of statistics about a variety of subjects

Atlases: collections of maps

Bibliographies: lists of works published about specific topics

Dictionaries: reference works that provide the pronunciations and definitions of words

Encyclopedias: reference works that provide information on many different topics

Specialized encyclopedias: encyclopedias of articles related to a single general topic, such as art or medicine

WIKIPEDIA

Wikipedia is a source you might come across in your preliminary research. It's a free, open-source, online encyclopedia with articles about nearly every topic imaginable. Open-source means two things. First, it means that the site itself and all the information on it were added by users. Wikipedia articles can be written and edited by anyone—from experts to amateurs. This means that not all the information in Wikipedia articles is reliable. Second, open-source means that a product is free for anyone to use. You don't need to pay or look at paid advertising to access the information on this website.

Like other encyclopedias, Wikipedia can be good for getting a general overview of your topic. It can direct you to keywords or lead you to ask new questions. The best Wikipedia articles have extensive bibliographies, so make note of any sources that could lead to further information. But don't use Wikipedia as your sole source for anything—be sure to check any facts against other sources.

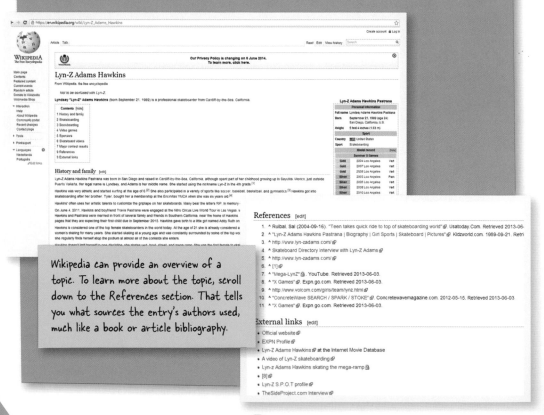

Wikipedia can provide an overview of a topic. To learn more about the topic, scroll down to the References section. That tells you what sources the entry's authors used, much like a book or article bibliography.

As you read reference articles on your topic, note any keywords that pop up a lot. These words are likely important and might be worth looking up as you continue your research. Also, look at the bibliography entries at the end of an article. These are the sources the author used in researching the article. They might have more information on your topic. So keep a list of the ones that might be useful for further research.

ONLINE SOURCES

Once you have a general overview of your topic, you're ready to dig a little deeper. Think about your assignment and the types of information you are looking for. Are you researching a recent event—something that happened in the last few months? Then there probably aren't any books about it yet. But maybe it was covered in the news. You could probably find online articles and possibly even videos. Are you researching something that happened long ago, such as World War II? Then you can probably find books about it. You might even be able to access old newspaper articles and photographs. And there may be entire websites dedicated to the topic.

Of course, you can find something about nearly *every* subject on the Internet. In fact, you can usually find a lot of somethings. Try doing an online search for your topic. Do you get about 60 million results? That's a lot of somethings. On most search engines, the most relevant results are listed first. But you should be aware that the first two or three websites listed might be from companies that have paid to have their sites come up first. Those listings are often ads intended to get you to buy a product. They might be displayed in a separate box or labeled with the word *ad* or *sponsored.* Unless you are researching a specific product or company, these results probably won't be the most useful ones for your project.

What if you want to see what something looks or sounds like? Videos, images, and audio files can be great sources of information. If you are learning about an artist, for instance, you will better understand his importance if you look at examples of his work. Many search engines allow you to search specifically for images. So if you want to see examples of Vincent van Gogh's paintings, you might search for "Vincent van Gogh" and then click on the search engine's Images option.

Most search engines let you search specifically for videos too. A video can show you exactly what happened at an event or what someone looks or sounds like. In a video of a concert, you can see and hear what a musician wore, how the musician performed and interacted with the crowd, and how the crowd responded.

DON'T FORGET THE LIBRARY

No matter how many sources you find online, you'll probably also need some books about your topic. Perhaps you even found some titles online and want to get your hands on them. It's time to use the library again.

The first step is to look up your topic in the library's online catalog. You can do this either in the library or from the comfort of your own home. You might search the catalog for a specific title or author. This is most useful if you are looking for specific sources

Hennepin County Library home · Internet · catalog · locations & hours · library cards · my account · ask us

KID Links

kidlinks home · homework help · books & reading · library events · fun & games

home > homework help > history

history

DATABASES

America the Beautiful
Offers state history and current events. Includes images, maps, a timeline, quizzes and games. For elementary and middle school students.

American Indian Experience
Offers articles as well as primary documents, including treaties, speeches, traditional tales, maps and photos.

FreedomFlix
Explore significant events in history using Scholastic's Cornerstones of Freedom book series. You can watch videos, read books online and other related material, visit recommended websites, do a project, and answer questions about your topic.

Grolier Multimedia Encyclopedia
An encyclopedia of articles, images, maps, sound and multimedia. Research System offers su...
research...

WEBSITES

African American Registry
An encyclopedia of African American people and heritage. Search by keyword, category or by name.

America's Story
Famous Americans, the 50 states and more. Jump back in time to your birth date. From the Library of Congress.

Ben's Guide to Government
Information about how government works. Organized by grade level. From the U.S. Government.

Black History
Photos and information about famous African-Americans, plus links to books, timelines, places in history and more.

Countries & States
Find information about any country or state in the U.S.

Hispanic Heritage
Meet famous Latinos and learn about Hispanic history in the Americas.

Native American Websites
...
Native ...ibrary, OR.
Kids

Many school and public libraries offer access to kid-friendly research databases.

gleaned from the bibliography of another work or from an Internet search. Or you can search by keyword. Try some terms from your list of keywords.

You might also check databases of newspaper, magazine, and journal articles. These databases work much like a library catalog. But instead of cataloging books, they index articles. Like library catalogs, databases can be searched by author, title, or keyword. Many databases will give you the full text of articles. Others include only an abstract, or a summary. But your library might have ways for you to get the full text in print or on microform. Check with your librarian.

CHAPTER 5

WHAT ARE PRIMARY AND SECONDARY SOURCES?

There's one more thing to consider as you search for sources. Your teacher may require you to use a combination of primary and secondary sources. Primary sources reveal firsthand information. They include autobiographies, eyewitness accounts, news stories about an event (written or recorded at the time of the event), photographs, and even the words of a poem or letter. Primary sources can also include research you conduct yourself: interviews, surveys, experiments, and observations.

Secondary sources, on the other hand, present an analysis or interpretation of primary sources. So a book about an event that wasn't written by an eyewitness to the event is a secondary source. Encyclopedia articles are secondary sources too. A news article that analyzes an event after it happened is also a secondary source.

Neither primary nor secondary sources are better. Primary sources can offer you a firsthand account of what the people

involved in an event thought or saw or felt. Secondary sources can help provide some perspective on that event. For example, eyewitness accounts of the Boston Marathon bombing in 2013 can help you to understand the fear and horror of that day. But books written in the years that followed the attack can provide perspective on why it occurred, as well as what worked and what didn't in the emergency response. So as you are gathering sources, be sure to look for both primary and secondary sources of information.

But wait—your search for sources isn't necessarily done yet. Depending on your topic, it might be time to make your own clues!

DO-IT-YOURSELF RESEARCH

In addition to searching for sources in libraries and online, don't overlook the possibility of carrying out your own research in the form of observations, experiments, surveys, or interviews. Sometimes your teacher will require you to conduct your own research. If that's not the case but you think independent research would improve your project, be sure to ask your teacher first.

Let's say you are writing about how young children share (or don't share). You could go to your local park and watch how children take turns on the playground. Or you could go to a day care (with permission) and observe how children share toys.

Before you go, be sure to plan what you will observe. Are you going to watch children of a certain age group? Are you only interested in examples of how they share? Or do you want to know how they react when someone doesn't share? Be sure to take notes about your observations. It can be helpful to make observations on more than one occasion or in more than one location as well.

Research projects for a science class often involve setting up your own experiment. Perhaps you want to test what color light plants grow best under. Then you might plant several seeds and keep them under different-colored lightbulbs. You could take measurements of plant growth each day. Again, be sure to record your results.

While science often involves experimentation, projects for social studies might require you to find out more about what people think. You can do this with a survey. Your survey can include yes or no questions, such as this one: Have you ever cheated on a test? Or you can write multiple-choice questions. An example might be the following: How many times have you cheated on a test this year? (a) 0, (b) 1–5, (c) 5–10, (d) 10 or more.

Or you can write open-ended questions, allowing participants to write their own answers, such as this question: How do you feel about cheating? Afterward, tally your survey results to see how participants responded.

For some topics, an interview can be a rich source of information. This is especially true if you are writing a biography of someone who is living. Who better to tell you about that person than himself?

Or you might interview an expert on your topic. If you're writing about how to care for a new puppy, you might interview a veterinarian. It's possible to find contact information for almost anyone online. But before you start firing off questions, it is polite to contact the person and request an interview. She will probably be flattered! (But if she declines the interview, thank her for her response and move on.)

You can conduct your interview via e-mail, over the phone, or in person. No matter how you do it, though, be sure to think of questions ahead of time and write them down. If you think of more questions during the interview, go ahead and add them. Be sure to take notes or record the interview (with the subject's permission). And always end by saying thank you.

So you have sources—a *lot* of sources! Now what do you do with them?

CHAPTER 6

HOW DO I START SELECTING SOURCES?

Just as a detective writes down clues, you should write down information about your potential sources as you find them. You do this in a working bibliography. *Bibliography* is just a fancy name for a list of sources. And a working bibliography is just what it sounds like—a bibliography that hasn't been finalized yet. You will add to it and subtract from it as you go. Whenever you find a source that looks promising, add it to your working bibliography.

In your working bibliography, include information that will help you identify the work and find it again later. For books, this includes the author, the title, the place of publication, the publisher, and the year published. Also jot down the call number—the book's "address" on the library shelf—so that you can find it easily. For journal, magazine, and newspaper articles, note the author, the article's title, the publication, the volume and the issue number (if they are listed), and the date of publication. For a magazine or journal, also write down the page numbers of the article. Websites can be a little harder to record. Many do not list an author or a date. But include as much information as you can find: author, website title, sponsoring organization, date updated, and URL. Some teachers will also require you to note the date you accessed the site.

You might also note on your working bibliography what each source covers, such as "Discusses the history of origami," or "Benjamin Franklin's childhood." Then when you're looking for specific information, you'll know which source to check. As you research, you might find that some of your sources are not as useful as you anticipated. No problem. Just cross them off the list. You might also find that the bibliography at the end of a book or an article includes sources that aren't on your list yet. What are you waiting for? Add them!

SAMPLE WORKING BIBLIOGRAPHY

Subject: Women in the Military

Miller, Mary, and Karen Zeinert. *The Brave Women of the Gulf Wars.* Minneapolis: Twenty-First Century Books, 2006.
Profiles three women in the Gulf Wars and offers a history of the wars

Rudow, Barbara. *Yes She Did! Military.* La Jolla, CA: Scobre Educational, 2014.
Follows the history of women's roles in the military

"Today's Women Soldiers." *Women in the U.S. Army.* Army.mil Features. no date.
http://www.army.mil/women/today.html.
Statistics about women in the US Army from the 1980s to 2013

The best part is that your working bibliography will eventually morph into your final bibliography. So cite your sources following the format your teacher has asked you to use. There! That's one less step you have to worry about down the road!

NARROW DOWN THE OPTIONS

But wait! Is your working bibliography really long? Like how-could-I-ever-read-this-many-sources-before-my-deadline long? Don't panic! It's time to narrow down your sources.

That sounds easy enough, right? Maybe you'll just throw out every third one. Well, there's a little more to it than that. You want to narrow down the sources to the ones that will likely be the most useful to you. But without reading through every source on your list, how can you possibly know?

First, think back to your research question and your preliminary thesis. You want sources that can help answer your question and support your thesis. So you want relevant sources. If you're writing about turkeys, then a book about chickens probably won't help. Sometimes, though, relevance is more subtle than that. If you are writing about boating safety, a book about water safety may or may not include your topic.

A source might also include information that is related to your topic but doesn't address your specific research question. Unless you want to change your research question and

Gov't & Court Documents   PRINT THIS DOCUMENT
Indian Civil Rights Act (1968)   EMAIL THIS DOCUMENT
                                                 CITE THIS DOCUMENT

This federal legislation, enacted with the Omnibus Civil Rights Act of 1968 on April 11, 1968, specifically delineated the civil rights of Indians as protected by the U.S. Constitution and recognized by the federal government. The act also extended certain provisions of the Constitution to Indian tribes. Below is an excerpt of the act.

Title II. Rights of Indians

Section 210. Definitions

For purposes of this title, the term:

(1) "Indian tribe" means any tribe, band, or other group of Indians subject to the jurisdiction of the United States and recognized as possessing powers of self-government;

(2) "powers of self-government" means and includes all governmental powers possessed by an Indian tribe, executive, legislative, and judicial, and all offices, bodies, and tribunals by and through which they are executed ... arts of

Related Entries

EVENTS
FOURTEENTH AMENDMENT
INDIAN CIVIL RIGHTS ACT OF 1968

> You can use the Find command to search an article or database page for key terms. If your key terms come up a lot, it's probably a good source for your project.

your preliminary thesis, you can pass this information by. To find out what a book covers, look at its description in the library catalog. That description might even include the book's table of contents.

For articles or websites, skim the abstract, if there is one. Look for subheadings too. These can tell you what each section of an article is about. Or check different pages of the website. You might even consider searching a page's content to find how often key terms pop up. (Most web browsers allow you to do this using the Find command, or Control-F.) Weed out any books, articles, or sites that don't appear to be relevant to your topic.

You might also look at the publication dates of the sources on your list. Are some of your secondary sources more than ten or twenty years old? Are you comparing thoughts about your topic from that time period with thoughts on the topic today? If not, these older sources may not be useful, especially if your subject is medicine or technology. Older primary sources, such as autobiographies, newspaper articles, or photographs, may still help you, though, so be sure to keep them on your list!

MOVING ON

With your narrowed-down working bibliography in hand, you are ready to move on to the next phase of your research project. But look how far you've come already! You've gone from figuring out your assignment to picking a topic. You've conducted preliminary research and narrowed down your sources. If you can do that, you can do the rest of your assignment. After all, you now have a pile of information at your fingertips.

Not only that, but you also know how to find information. And that is a skill you'll use throughout your life, to look up movie listings and more! Congratulations. You are a researcher!

NOW YOU DO IT

Time to try out your new skills! Your assignment: Choose a research topic that is not too broad and not too narrow—one that is just right. Start by making a list or an idea web of some topics that interest you. Pick one or two that might be fun to research. Come up with two or three keywords for each topic. Do a quick search in a library catalog to see how many resources are available. If there are too many, narrow your topic further. Are there too few? Think bigger. Once you have chosen your just-right topic, come up with some research questions. Make a list of the types of information you will need to answer them.

GLOSSARY

bibliography: a list of sources used in preparing a research project

call number: a series of numbers and letters, based on a book's subject or author, that designates the book's location on a library shelf

database: an electronic collection of articles or information organized in ways that allow for searching and sorting

debate: a discussion or contest in which two sides present opposing viewpoints of a subject

illustration: an example that helps make an idea or concept clearer

journal: a magazine about a specific subject or industry. Journal articles are often scholarly in nature.

microform: tiny images of document pages. A special machine is used to make the images large enough to read.

persuade: to convince someone that a certain viewpoint is correct or to take a certain action

preliminary: an early stage of a project. When something is preliminary, it is not final.

synonym: a word that has the same (or similar) meaning as another word

thesaurus: a reference work that lists synonyms

SELECTED BIBLIOGRAPHY

Ballenger, Bruce. *The Curious Researcher: A Guide to Writing Research Papers*. New York: Pearson Longman, 2004.

Gibaldi, Joseph. *MLA Handbook for Writers of Research Papers*. New York: Modern Language Association of America, 2003.

How to Write a Great Research Paper. San Francisco: John Wiley & Sons, 2004.

Lester, James D., Jr., and James D. Lester Sr. *Research Paper Handbook*. Tucson: Good Year Books, 2005.

Taylor, Gordon. *A Student's Writing Guide: How to Plan and Write Successful Essays*. Cambridge: Cambridge University Press, 2009.

Turabian, Kate. *A Manual for Writers of Research Papers, Theses, and Dissertations*. Chicago: University of Chicago Press, 2013.

LERNER

SOURCE

Expand learning beyond the printed book. Download free, complementary educational resources for this book from our website, www.lerneresource.com.

FURTHER INFORMATION

Bodden, Valerie. *Assess and Select Your Sources*. Minneapolis: Lerner Publications, 2015. This book guides you through the challenge of assessing how reliable and useful your potential sources really are.

Classzone: Web Research Guide
http://www.classzone.com/books/research_guide/page_build.cfm?state=none&CFID=43318372&CFTOKEN=34434752
Take a quiz to find out how much you already know about using the Internet for research. Then learn even more skills to make you the best researcher around!

Fact Monster
http://www.factmonster.com
This subject directory, designed just for young researchers, has links to all kinds of topics!

Fontichiaro, Kristin, and Emily Johnson. *Know What to Ask: Forming Great Research Questions*. Ann Arbor, MI: Cherry Lake, 2013. Learn how to write the best research questions for your project.

The Kentucky Virtual Library Presents: How to Do Research
http://www.kyvl.org/kids/homebase.html
This library-sponsored site walks you through the steps of a research project, starting with choosing your topic and ending with evaluating your final product.

KidsClick!
http://www.kidsclick.org
Looking for a topic? This subject directory was designed by librarians, just for young researchers like you! Browse the subjects to see if one sparks your interest.

INDEX

PHOTO ACKNOWLEDGMENTS

The images in this book are used with the permission of: © Vitaly Korovin/Shutterstock, p. 4 (top left); © Carolyn Franks/Shutterstock, pp. 5 (top), 10 (top left); © iStockphoto/Devonyu, p. 6 (top left); © iStockphoto/mphillips007, p. 7; © Anton Gvozdikov/Shutterstock, p. 8; © iStockphoto/malerapaso, p. 11 (top right); © iStockphoto/PacoRomero, p. 12; © Website The Regents of the University of Michigan and Drexel University, p. 13; NASA, ESA, and H. Richer (University of British Columbia), p. 14; © iStockphoto/digitalfarmer, p. 15; © iStockphoto/Suzifoo, p. 16; © Rozaliya/Dreamstime, p. 17; National Archives 111-B-168, p. 18; © Fouroaks/Dreamstime, p. 19; © Ryan Balderas/E+/Getty Images, p. 20; © Tim Greenway/Portland Press Herald via Getty Images, p. 21; © iStockphoto/sd619, pp. 22, 23 (top); © Romica/Dreamstime, p. 23 (bottom); Wikipedia, p. 24; Website © Hennepin County Library, pp. 27, 35; © Derek Burke/Dreamstime, p. 28; © iStockphoto/ginosphotos, p. 29; © iStockphoto/Elenathewise, p. 30; © iStockphoto/kali9, p. 31; © Berit Kessler/Shutterstock, p. 32; © iStockphoto/Gravicapa, p. 34.

Cover and interior backgrounds: © koosen/Shutterstock (brown background); © Mrs. Opossum/Shutterstock (zig zag pattern); © AKSANA SHUM/Shutterstock (diamond pattern); © AtthameeNi/Shutterstock (blue lined graph paper); © Looper/Shutterstock (arrows); © AlexanderZam/Shutterstock (graph paper dots); © oleschwander/Shutterstock (yellow lined paper dots).